THE OFFICIAL ANNUAL 2022

WRITTEN BY STEVE BARTRAM
DESIGNED BY DANIEL JAMES

g

A Grange Publication

© 2021. Published by Grange Communications Ltd, Edinburgh, under
licence from Manchester United Football Club. Printed in the EU.

Photography © MUFC.

ISBN: 978-1-913578-78-7

CONTENTS

WELCOME

TO THE 2022 MANCHESTER UNITED ANNUAL!

You might know the Reds inside out, but this is where you can get even deeper inside the greatest club in English football.

In addition to profiles of some of your favourite players in the men's and women's squads, you can also get to know the pro gamers who represent United in the world of esports, plus enjoy an introduction to Zac and Charlie, AKA the Little Devils, the club's newest reporters.

The hard-hitting questions continue through an epic series of Q&A sessions where first team stars tackle posers from supporters, while we also look back on the Reds' biggest ever Premier League wins and delve into what it takes to make the grade as a youngster at Old Trafford.

There's all of this and more besides in the 2022 Manchester United Annual. To see how well you know the Reds, you can test your knowledge with a stack of tricky quizzes and teasers, before entering our competition to win a Reds shirt signed by men's squad members!

Enjoy, and keep the Red flag flying high!

2021/22 REVIEWED

In Ole Gunnar Solskjaer's second full season as United manager, the Reds continued to improve, making progress in the Premier League and coming within a penalty shootout of winning a major European trophy…

PREMIER LEAGUE

2ND PLACE

Having finished third in 2019/20, expectations were high for United going into the new season. However, the impact of the COVID-19 pandemic continued to be felt as the Reds were unable to put together a pre-season campaign, and therefore had to play catch-up on the division's other teams from opening day. Three defeats in the opening six games made matters even tougher, but Solskjaer's side went on a sensational run of form after that to put themselves right in the title race and, by mid-January, United were on top of the table. Unfortunately, dropped points in late January and February proved costly at the same time that Manchester City were putting together a relentless winning run. By the time the sides met in March's Manchester derby at the Etihad Stadium, the title race was all but done – however, the Reds demonstrated their ability to beat any team by putting together a comfortable 2-0 win over Pep Guardiola's Blues. City did recover to take the title in the end, but United still ended the campaign with second place comfortably locked up, while also posting a new club record by going undefeated away from home for the entire league season. Year on year, the Reds continue to rise…

TAKE ME HOME UNITED ROAD

EUROPE 🏆🏆

An unkind Champions League group stage draw put the Reds up against two of the previous season's four semi-finalists – PSG and RB Leipzig – plus Turkish champions Istanbul Basaksehir. With four games gone and three wins secured, including another late win in Paris, the Reds looked set for the knockout stages, only for two narrow defeats to consign Solskjaer's side to third place and a spot in the Europa League.

Rather than sulk about exiting the Champions League, United quickly rattled through the competition, bypassing Real Sociedad, AC Milan and Granada before obliterating AS Roma in the semi-finals with a thrilling 8-5 aggregate victory which set up a final against Villarreal in Gdansk. There, a tense 1-1 draw preceded a heart-breaking penalty shootout defeat for the Reds, who picked up invaluable experience of the continental game.

FA CUP 🏆

QUARTER-FINALISTS

After overcoming promotion hopefuls Watford in the third round, United were handed a barnstorming fourth round encounter with Liverpool at Old Trafford and duly edged an absolute classic, winning 3-2 courtesy of Bruno Fernandes's brilliant late free-kick. The tough draws kept on coming, with West Ham overcome in M16 after extra-time, before the Reds' run in the competition came to an end with a 3-1 defeat at Leicester in the last eight. The Foxes, of course, went on to win the trophy with a 1-0 win over Chelsea at Wembley.

LEAGUE CUP 🏆

SEMI-FINALISTS

For the second year in a row, United reached the last four of the League Cup before exiting to eventual winners Manchester City. The Reds didn't concede a goal in the third, fourth or fifth rounds, comfortably overpowering Luton Town and Brighton before patiently wearing down Everton in the quarter-finals just before Christmas. A pair of goals conceded from set-pieces proved United's undoing in the last four, however, leaving the Reds agonisingly short of another return to Wembley Stadium.

YOUR 2020/21 AWARD WINNERS

At the end of every season, United's players through the ranks are recognised with a series of individual honours – here's who picked up silverware after a sterling season's work in 2020/21...

SIR MATT BUSBY PLAYER OF THE YEAR

BRUNO FERNANDES

VOTED BY SUPPORTERS

A staggering 28 goals scored and 18 assisted represented an insane campaign for United's Portuguese playmaker, who retained the Sir Matt Busby Player of the Year award he won for his first half-season at Old Trafford in 2019/20.

As such, only David De Gea (four times) and Cristiano Ronaldo (three times) have won the trophy more times than Bruno, which is sensational considering that it took him just 16 months to win it twice!

"Individual trophies are really good for players," he grinned. "It lifts you up. It means that the people are liking you, like the way you play, the way you are trying to help the team, the way you do things, so that's very important for me."

TRIVIA The top three players in the supporters' poll picked up 90% of all votes cast, with Bruno notching 63%, Luke Shaw picking up 21% and Edinson Cavani taking 6%.

PLAYERS' PLAYER OF THE YEAR

LUKE SHAW

VOTED BY UNITED'S FIRST TEAM SQUAD

Winning the approval of your fellow players is not easy, and Luke Shaw picked up the Players' Player of the Year award for the second time in three seasons to underline just how much his team-mates appreciate his contribution to the team.

With the most appearances of his Reds career to date, plus a series of key assists and a brilliant clinching Manchester derby clinching-goal at the Etihad Stadium, 2020/21 comfortably represented Luke's best season as a United player.

Explaining why he voted for the England international defender, Aaron Wan-Bissaka said: "Luke has been the standout for me. He's been positive throughout, making the most of every game. He's not taken his foot off the pedal."

TRIVIA Luke is only the fourth player to win the award more than once, after Cristiano Ronaldo (2006/07, 2008/09), Antonio Valencia (2011/12, 2016/17) and David De Gea (2013/14, 2014/15, 2017/18).

GOAL OF THE SEASON

BRUNO FERNANDES V EVERTON

Everything you could ever want to know about Bruno Fernandes's game was there to see in his spectacular goal against Everton at Old Trafford. There was the swagger as he dummied the ball, allowing it to reach Aaron Wan-Bissaka, then more trickery as he shifted the ball wide of Toffees midfielder Tom Davies, then unreal power, skill and audacity as he cracked a 20-yarder into the far top corner. Ludicrous.

TRIVIA

Bruno's goals occupied the top two slots in the final ranking, with his long-ranger against the Toffees just about edging out his magnificent counter-attacking effort at Newcastle.

VOTED BY SUPPORTERS

VOTED BY UNITED WOMEN'S COACHING STAFF AND PLAYERS

WOMEN'S PLAYER OF THE YEAR

ONA BATLLE

As debut campaigns go, Ona Batlle's first season at United Women takes some beating. The Spanish international joined from Levante in the summer of 2020 and quickly played her way into first team regularity. A consistently impressive performer in either full-back position, Ona played a major role in 10 clean sheets across her 23 appearances and continued to earn international recognition with a string of caps for Spain.

"I have no words to describe how grateful I am for everything I experienced this year," she said after collecting her award. "It's been a very special first year, but now we have to look ahead and continue learning and improving what we've done."

TRIVIA

Ona is the first-ever non-British recipient of the award, following on from previous winners Katie Zelem in 2018/19 and Hayley Ladd in 2019/20.

DENZIL HAROUN U23S PLAYER OF THE YEAR

HANNIBAL MEJBRI

VOTED BY U23S COACH NEIL WOOD

The 2020/21 campaign was a major one for teenage playmaker Hannibal Mejbri, who clocked up 13 goal involvements in 21 outings for the Reds' Under-23s, made his first team debut on the final day of the Premier League season and committed his international future to Tunisia before going on to make his senior international bow. Talk about cramming a lot in! An outstanding season prompted coach Neil Wood to name him Player of the Year, to which Hannibal admitted: "I learned a lot. I had to be stronger. I was more consistent in the games and I had more goals and assists than the season before. It's always good to take that step."

VOTED BY U18S COACH NEIL RYAN

JIMMY MURPHY YOUNG PLAYER OF THE YEAR

SHOLA SHORETIRE

So impressive was Shola Shoretire's form in United's youth ranks, that in 2021 he became the seventh youngest player in United's history and the 240th Academy graduate to make his first team debut. The quick-witted forward, who came on in the win over Newcastle, shone in every age group he represented, deservedly winning the Under-18s Player of the Year award and emulating the likes of fellow graduates Mason Greenwood and Marcus Rashford. "Seeing I'm on the same path that they were on as well, shows how well United are doing through the Academy and getting people into the first team," noted Shola.

11

PLAYER PROFILES

Throughout the Annual we'll be profiling a selection of Reds from across Ole's first-team squad, kicking off with Tom and Victor…

TOM HEATON

22

RETURNING RED

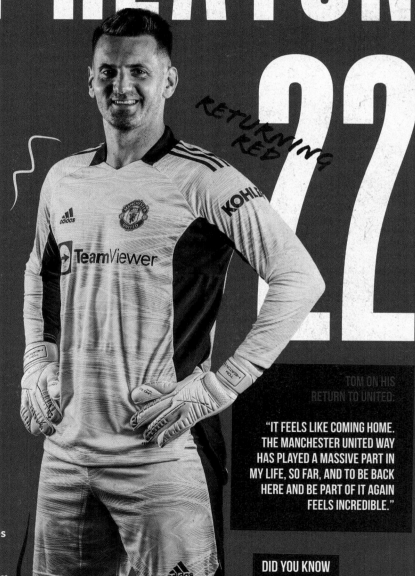

"FOR TOM TO COME IN AND TAKE HIS CHALLENGE IS WHAT HE NEEDED, IT'S THAT LAST STEP NOW. HE'S SUCH A TOP PROFESSIONAL AND SUCH A TOP GUY TO HAVE AROUND AND THAT WILL HELP THE YOUNG LADS."

OLE GUNNAR SOLSKJAER, JULY 2021

POSITION: GOALKEEPER
BORN: 15 APRIL 1986; CHESTER, ENGLAND

After rising up through United's Academy and embarking on a series of successful loans, Tom Heaton left Old Trafford in 2010 to make a first-team career. Spells with Cardiff and Bristol City preceded a move to Burnley, where Tom shone at Premier League level and earned three England call-ups. Following two years at Aston Villa, Heaton completed a shock return to the Reds on a free transfer in 2021.

TOM ON HIS RETURN TO UNITED:

"IT FEELS LIKE COMING HOME. THE MANCHESTER UNITED WAY HAS PLAYED A MASSIVE PART IN MY LIFE, SO FAR, AND TO BE BACK HERE AND BE PART OF IT AGAIN FEELS INCREDIBLE."

DID YOU KNOW

TOM IS ONLY THE FIFTH YOUTH SYSTEM GRADUATE TO LEAVE UNITED AND SUBSEQUENTLY REJOIN THE CLUB, AFTER MARK HUGHES, MARK BOSNICH, PAUL SCHOLES AND PAUL POGBA.

FOCUS ON...

VICTOR LINDELOF

"VICTOR'S A THINKING DEFENDER. HE'S SOMEONE WHO LIKES TO READ AND COVER - HE'S TAKEN ON THAT RESPONSIBILITY AND THAT SUITS HIM."
EX-UNITED DEFENDER RIO FERDINAND, JUNE 2021

VICTOR ON HIS STYLE OF LEADERSHIP:

"ON THE PITCH, I TRY TO BE A LEADER THROUGH THE WAY I PLAY. THAT COULD BE PLAYING OUT FROM THE BACK, GOING IN FOR A BIG TACKLE OR TO RELAX THE GAME DOWN BY TAKING MORE TIME ON THE BALL. I'M MORE OF A LEADER IN THAT WAY."

ICE MAN

POSITION: CENTRE-BACK
BORN: 17 JULY 1994;
VASTERAS, SWEDEN

A cool, calm central defender who has improved year-on-year since his 2017 arrival from Benfica, Victor Lindelof is capable of turning in his best performances in the Reds' biggest games. Totally unfazed by pressure, the laid-back Swedish international likes to use his insightful reading of the game to stay one step ahead of opposing forwards.

DID YOU KNOW?

IN 2019, AS PART OF A SPONSORSHIP DEAL WITH THE SWEDISH NATIONAL TEAM, VICTOR AND INTERNATIONAL TEAM-MATE JOHN GUIDETTI TATTOOED A SUPPORTER. THE DUO INKED THEIR INITIALS AND A PAIR OF BINOCULARS ON THE ARM OF FAN ANDERS THORNVALL, WHO LOVED THEIR ARTWORK!

13

EPIC VICTORIES!

During the course of 2020/21, the Reds equalled the biggest win in Premier League history with the 9-0 obliteration of Southampton at Old Trafford. Here, we run through United's five biggest wins since the competition began...

HE GOES BY THE NAME OF WAYNE ROONEY!

8-2

AUGUST 2011 VS ARSENAL (H)

Arsene Wenger's side were missing a lot of players through injury, but that didn't lessen the shock of United's huge win. After Danny Welbeck's opener, Ashley Young and Wayne Rooney both notched two spectacular hits apiece, then Rooney completed his hat-trick from the spot. Nani and Ji-sung Park also struck, with Theo Walcott and Robin van Persie replying for the meek Gunners.

7-0

OCTOBER 1997 VS BARNSLEY (H)

GOAL KING COLE!

Another big win, another hat-trick, this time for Andy Cole, who was in unstoppable form against the Tykes. The same applied to Ryan Giggs, who hit a sensational solo goal, as did Paul Scholes. Giggs also bagged a second before Czech Republic star Karel Poborsky rounded off the scoring late on with a cheeky backheel.

YOU ARE MY SOLSKJAER!

8-1

FEBRUARY 1999 VS NOTTINGHAM FOREST (A)

Until Leicester's 9-0 win at 10-man Southampton in 2019, this was the Premier League's biggest-ever away win – though it remains one of the most remarkable substitute displays ever. United led 4-1 with 10 minutes left, thanks to pairs from Andy Cole and Dwight Yorke, before Ole Gunnar Solskjaer entered from the bench and duly smashed in four goals in no time at all. Sensational!

HE GETS THE BALL AND SCORES A GOAL, ANDY, ANDY COLE!

9-0

MARCH 1995 VS IPSWICH TOWN (H)

Once again, that man Andy Cole played a starring role, bagging five goals in a record rout of the Tractor Boys at Old Trafford. Roy Keane opened the scoring, but Cole then took over by rattling off five close-range efforts, while Mark Hughes notched twice and Paul Ince chipped in – literally – with a cheeky free-kick into an open goal!

TELL ME HOW GOOD DOES IT FEEL!

9-0

FEBRUARY 2021 VS SOUTHAMPTON (H)

Not only a record-equalling margin of victory, but also a club record achievement of seven United players scoring in the same game. After Alexandre Jankewitz was sent off less than two minutes in, only Anthony Martial scored more than once for the Reds, as Aaron Wan-Bissaka, Marcus Rashford, Edinson Cavani, Bruno Fernandes (from the spot), Scott McTominay and Daniel James netted, while Jan Bednarek scored at the wrong end on a miserable night for the Saints.

REINTRODUCING...

CRISTIANO RONALDO

In August 2021, over 18 years after first moving to United as a teenager, Cristiano Ronaldo rejoined the Reds from Juventus in one of the most sensational transfers in football history. Now that the Portuguese megastar has returned home, here's a reminder of some of the highlights of his first stint with United...

2003
Shortly after David Beckham departed Old Trafford, United faced Sporting Lisbon in a pre-season friendly. The Reds were already aware of Cristiano's ability after scouting him for years, but his brilliant display in Sporting's 3-1 win persuaded Sir Alex Ferguson to sign him that same night!

2004
After a promising debut season in English football, Ronaldo capped his campaign with the opening goal in the 2004 FA Cup final as United beat Millwall 3-0. After one season, he was already picking up silverware!

2006
Finishing his third campaign in fine form, Cristiano smashed home United's third goal in the League Cup final win over Wigan Athletic, a success which laid the foundations for a hugely successful period in the club's history.

2007
In his breakthrough season, Ronaldo hit 23 goals in all competitions as United won the Premier League for the first time in four seasons, reached the Champions League semi-final and FA Cup final. He was also named Player of the Year by England's sports journalists and his fellow players.

2008
A ridiculous haul of 42 goals in 49 games propelled United to a Premier League and Champions League double, while also retaining his PFA and FWA Player of the Year awards. Going one better, Cristiano also won his first ever Ballon d'Or!

2009
Ronaldo's sixth season with the Reds proved to be his last for a while, as Real Madrid made him a world record £80 million signing at the season's end, but not before he'd nabbed a third straight Premier League title, plus winner's medals in the Club World Cup and League Cup.

SEVEN REASONS RONNY IS A FOOTBALL LEGEND

- ☑ 30 MAJOR TROPHIES, INCLUDING FIVE UEFA CHAMPIONS LEAGUES
- ☑ FIVE BALLON D'ORS AND FOUR GOLDEN SHOES
- ☑ MOST GOALS SCORED BY ANYBODY, EVER IN INTERNATIONAL FOOTBALL
- ☑ MOST GOALS AND ASSISTS IN UEFA CHAMPIONS LEAGUE HISTORY
- ☑ EUROPEAN CHAMPIONSHIP WINNING CAPTAIN WITH PORTUGAL
- ☑ TOP SCORER IN PREMIER LEAGUE, LA LIGA AND SERIE A SEASONS
- ☑ PLAYER OF THE YEAR AWARDS IN ENGLAND, SPAIN AND ITALY

FOCUS ON...

HARRY MAGUIRE

HARRY ON LEADERS IN UNITED'S SQUAD:

"FOR SURE, IT'S THE BEST LEADERSHIP GROUP I'VE BEEN INVOLVED IN AT A CLUB. WE HAVE A LOT OF SENIOR PROS AND YOU DON'T EVEN HAVE TO BE A SENIOR PRO TO BE A LEADER. IT RUBS OFF ON OTHER PEOPLE WHEN YOU HAVE A STRONG MENTALITY, A WINNING MENTALITY. THERE'S DEFINITELY A LOT OF LEADERS IN THE DRESSING ROOM."

"I THINK HARRY'S BEEN THE OUTSTANDING ENGLISH DEFENDER IN THE LEAGUE THIS SEASON. HE'S BEEN SUCH A BEDROCK."

ENGLAND MANAGER GARETH SOUTHGATE, JUNE 2021

OUR CAPTAIN!

5

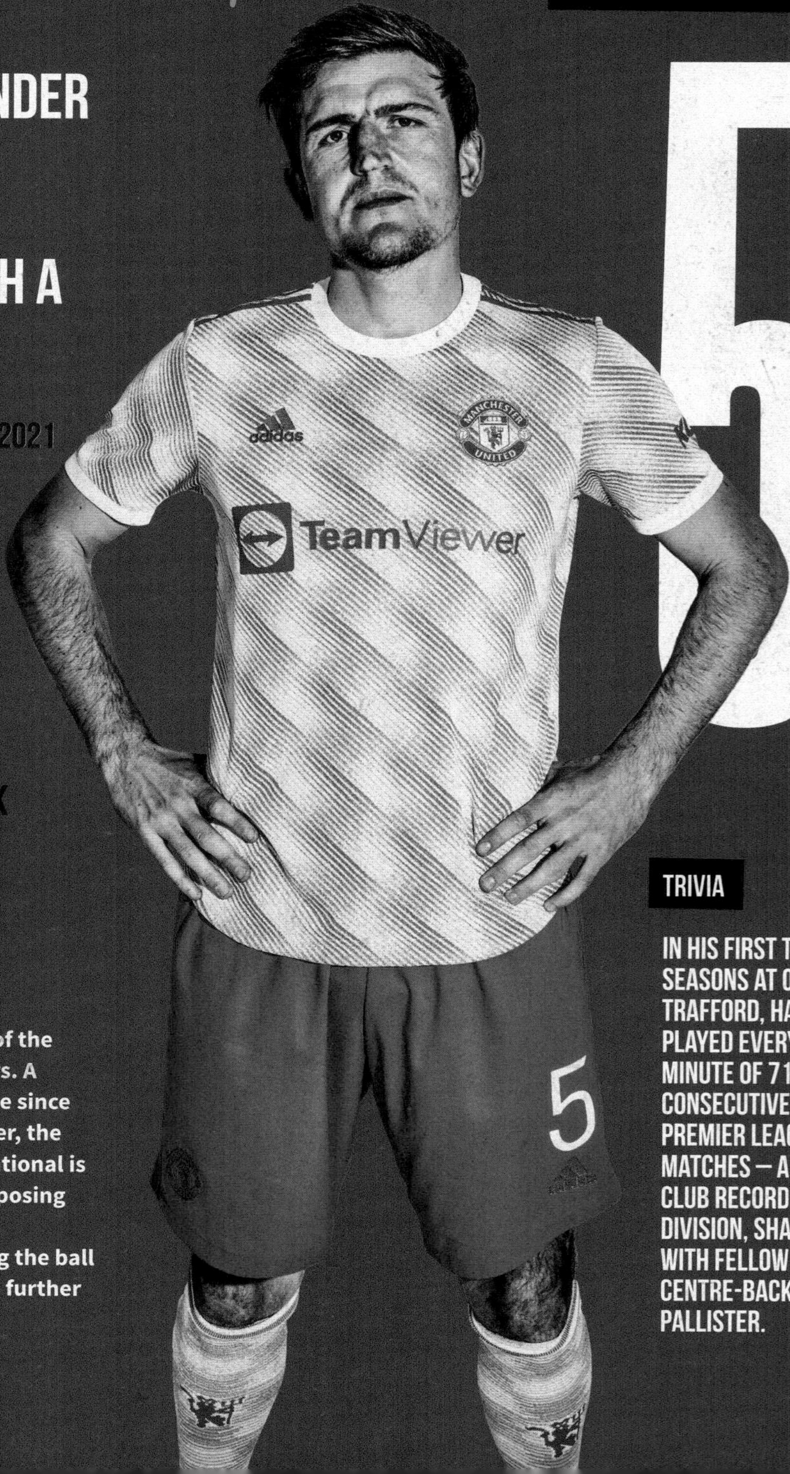

POSITION: CENTRE-BACK
BORN: 5 MARCH 1993; SHEFFIELD, ENGLAND

United's captain is also one of the Reds' most important players. A fixture in the heart of defence since his 2019 arrival from Leicester, the experienced England international is always one step ahead of opposing forwards, dominating them physically while also carrying the ball forward to help start attacks further up the field.

TRIVIA

IN HIS FIRST TWO SEASONS AT OLD TRAFFORD, HARRY PLAYED EVERY MINUTE OF 71 CONSECUTIVE PREMIER LEAGUE MATCHES – A JOINT CLUB RECORD IN THE DIVISION, SHARED WITH FELLOW CENTRE-BACK GARY PALLISTER.

LUKE SHAW

23

"LUKE SHAW IS STRONG. HE IS A BEAST, A BRICK. IF THERE'S ONE GUY I PLAY AGAINST THAT I KNOW IS GOING TO BE STRONG, IT'D DEFINITELY BE HIM."

ENGLAND INTERNATIONAL COLLEAGUE REECE JAMES, JUNE 2021

SHAWBERTO CARLOS

ON BEING NAMED PLAYERS' PLAYER OF THE YEAR BY HIS TEAM-MATES IN 2020/21:

"IT WAS MY BEST SEASON SO FAR. I NEED TO KEEP WORKING HARD, KEEP IMPROVING. I FEEL LIKE I CAN KEEP GETTING BETTER AND GIVE MORE FOR THE TEAM. SO, I NEED TO BE DOING THAT, KEEP GOING, KEEP MY HEAD DOWN AND WHAT WILL COME WILL COME."

POSITION: LEFT-BACK
BORN: 12 JULY 1995; KINGSTON-UPON-THAMES, ENGLAND

Luke Shaw is one of the longest-serving players in United's squad, having arrived from Southampton in 2014. Though he was named Sir Matt Busby Player of the Year in 2018/19, however, it's safe to say that 2020/21 was his finest season at Old Trafford to date, as his swashbuckling form up and down the left flank brought him an England recall and a spot in the PFA Team of the Year.

DID YOU KNOW?

DURING THE 2020/21 SEASON, LUKE'S FORM EARNED HIM COMPARISONS WITH LEGENDARY BRAZIL LEFT-BACK ROBERTO CARLOS, AND THE NICKNAME 'SHAWBERTO CARLOS'. LUKE'S RESPONSE? "I CAN'T BE COMPARED TO HIM, HE'S UNBELIEVABLE! I'M AWARE OF IT AND IT'S NICE TO BE EVEN MENTIONED ALONGSIDE HIS NAME, BUT I JUST LAUGH ABOUT IT!"

FANS'
QUESTIONS ANSWERED

SCOTT MCTOMINAY & MARCUS RASHFORD

They're used to facing the world's media, but how do these two homegrown Reds fare with questions from United fans from across the globe?

SCOTT MCTOMINAY

YOU JUMP EVERY TIME YOU WALK ONTO THE PITCH – IS THERE A REASON BEHIND THAT?

HANNAH G (UK)

"That's the first time someone has ever said and noticed me doing that! No, it's just to try to jump as high as I can to get ready, get the legs firing and get everything going. There is no superstition behind it. I just do it every game, it's not out of superstition. It's the same thing I do every time I get onto the pitch. I like to get warm and that's part of my routine."

WHAT DO YOU LIKE TO BE KNOWN AS? ARE YOU JUST CALLED SCOTTY AROUND THE TRAINING GROUND?

TARIK D (UK)

"Luke Shaw always says 'The Gym Man' because I'm always in the gym. But he always walks in when I'm in the gym so that's just a coincidence there. Other than that, Deano has got a few nicknames for me that are not really applicable and vice-versa for him. So, yeah, just Scotty. To be fair, all the coaches and all the players call me Scotty. Eric calls me McTerminator and he enjoys that one. He's a top guy, Eric."

WHICH ANIMAL DESCRIBES YOU THE BEST?

ALMA W (SWEDEN)

"An obvious one people say is I'm like a lion but it's the old cliché and such an easy one to pick. I would probably choose something a bit different. I'd probably say a killer whale. Whenever people think of the oceans, and the worst predators, they probably think great white sharks. It's the ones who come a little bit later, a little bit more ferocious, because the great white sharks are not actually that dangerous, so whenever you get in the water with an orca, a killer whale, you know you could be in trouble."

IN THE BIOPIC MOVIE OF YOUR LIFE, WHICH ACTOR WOULD YOU WANT TO PLAY YOU?

BEN C (UK)

"[Laughs] Who would I want to play me? Me. I'd be playing me. I'd be the actor. Maybe when I finish football, I might do a bit of acting."

↗ MAN UTD

WHAT IS THE BIGGEST AND MOST IMPACTFUL ADVICE FROM YOUR PARENTS THAT HAS STUCK WITH YOU UNTIL NOW?

NOEL A (INDONESIA)

"Whenever I was younger, it was more about enjoying it. Play with a smile on your face. Just go and enjoy playing football with your mates. I had brilliant friends growing up at Manchester United. Jack Harrison, Joe Riley, Callum Whelan, Dean Henderson. The names are endless. Cameron Borthwick-Jackson. All the boys I grew up with, we all enjoyed playing football together. We were so competitive and enjoyed that rush of adrenaline from competing with each other. You don't have time to get bogged down with tactics when you're a little kid just enjoying football."

IF YOU HAD TO START A BAND, WITH YOU BEING THE SINGER, WHO ELSE WOULD YOU CHOOSE?

SANTIAGO P (ARGENTINA)

"I would probably say… Axel can play piano. I would have me singing. Dan James dancing, even though he'd be just a little comedy act on the side. Then I'd have one more, we'd go with… Shawy. He can sing, I think. Me and Shawy duet, Axel on the piano and Jamo dancing."

AS A SCOT, IS IRN BRU YOUR GO-TO DRINK?

CONNOR R (UK)

"[Laughs] I do like Irn Brus. I like drinks that are freezing cold so every drink, I have to have it with ice. Me and Shawy, when we're in hotels, always need ice with our drinks. If it's a hot drink, it must be scalding hot. If I'm going to have a fizzy drink and Irn Bru is available, I would have that all day."

FANS' QUESTIONS ANSWERED

SCOTT McTOMINAY & MARCUS RASHFORD

MARCUS RASHFORD

HAVE YOU EVER RACED 100M BEFORE AND IF SO DO YOU KNOW YOUR FASTEST TIME?

DOREEN K (KENYA)

"I have run it before when I was young. I think it was 11 something, 11.4 maybe, but it was when I was quite young – 15 or 16. But, yeah, I enjoy athletics. I think a lot of what we do in football, the type of running we do, it's never straight line like a 100 metres. You've got to be able to chop and change direction and it's not something I practice a lot."

WHERE DID YOU GET ALL THOSE NUTMEG AND ELASTICO SKILLS? HOW MUCH PRACTICE GOES INTO THEM?

ELLY B (THAILAND)

"For me, when I'm on the pitch, I'm just enjoying myself. I try to play freely and try to open teams up in ways they're not expecting, just to create space and create chances. It's just me playing football really and what United have always allowed, me to express myself in that way on the pitch."

WHO DO YOU THINK WAS BETTER AT FREE-KICKS: BECKHAM OR CRISTIANO?

CHARLES N (KENYA)

"I would say Ronaldo probably as I've seen him more in my era and my generation. But then, at the same time, I've watched clips of Beckham and I remember, when I was really young, I used to watch him at Salford, at The Cliff, practising his technique. Even though they are two really different techniques, you have to respect both of them. They are both top free-kick takers so I'd probably choose Ronaldo, purely based on the fact I just got to see it live more."

OF ALL THE TATTOOS YOU HAVE, WHICH IS THE MOST SIGNIFICANT ONE TO YOU?

RAVICHAND M (SINGAPORE)

"My most significant tattoo is probably the one on my left arm for my nana, who died when I was younger. It's probably that one that means the most to me and that's why I've dedicated the most space to it."

DO YOU PREFER BEANS ON TOAST OR EGG ON TOAST?

ADEDOYIN A (NIGERIA)

"For me, it'll probably be eggs on toast. It's what I have for breakfast most of the time, some fried eggs on brown toast. For me, eggs on toast."

UNITED

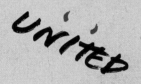

WHAT IS YOUR FAVOURITE BOOK?

KEITH P (UK)

"Hi Keith, my favourite book is called 'Relentless' and its more just for the mental side of things. I felt, when I read that book, it helped me to mature a lot and, in terms of sports, it made me a little bit more solid in my mentality. You can't let mistakes get to you. It's a 90-minute game and one mistake can drag out for 15 minutes and, before you know it, it's half-time and you've not been in the game for the last 10-15 minutes. So, yeah, I just try to stay focused. I like to read, to be honest, in my spare time, whether it's just a few pages or 20 pages, I just get a little bit of reading in as it's good for my mind."

CAN YOU SEE YOURSELF EVER ENTERING POLITICS, MARCUS?

MANC BORN AND BRED

ALLEN D (UK)

"The answer is no! I just feel like the people who want to do politics, it's what they dream of doing and the job they wanted to do from when they were young. I've been lucky enough to get the opportunity to live my dream through football and I think, after that, football is a draining game and a mentally challenging sport. So when I do retire, I'll just relax a little bit and then we'll see what happens."

INTRODUCING
JADON SANCHO

In July 2021, United completed the long-awaited transfer of skills wizard Jadon Sancho from Borussia Dortmund. The England winger is one of the most exciting signings in the Reds' recent history but, while his trickery is already world famous, let's get to know the man himself...

JADON ON... HIS CAGE FOOTBALL EDUCATION

"When I was younger, on my estate in South London, I just used to watch the older boys playing around and ever since then I just used to join in with them and started to fall in love with it, and then in school it was just always football and even after school it was just football. That's when it got serious. It was cage football – so when we saw the Ronaldinho adverts of him nutmegging people, that's what we tried to do."

JADON ON... HIS EARLY INFLUENCES

"Ronaldinho and obviously Wayne Rooney for England – those two are very iconic and great role models."

JADON ON... HIS UNITED IDOL

"Cristiano Ronaldo. What he's done in his career is a fantastic thing – where he started at Sporting and then he came to Manchester. So it's always good to see that all these iconic players have come through an iconic club."

JADON ON... HIS TATTOOS

"My first tattoo is also my most meaningful one, because my little brother passed away when he was younger and when I was in primary school I wrote a poem that I read at the funeral, so this one [on my left forearm] is definitely my most meaningful one. The rest around it are birds, heaven, an angel, a butterfly and then I have my sister's and my brother's initials. Then here [on my right forearm] I kind of freestyled, because I liked comics when I was younger. This isn't finished yet – obviously there's Spiderman, Sonic, The Simpsons…I haven't finished yet so there's more to come."

JADON ON... ENGLAND'S EURO 2020 CAMPAIGN

"It was obviously interesting. I didn't play as much as I would have liked to, but definitely to get a feeling of a major tournament was really important for me, especially given it was such a great group of lads. I will definitely take a lot away from that.

JADON ON... GOALS VS ASSISTS

"I feel like they're both as important as each other, because if you don't assist then where's it coming from?! You're kind of scoring the goal when you assist and then you've scored a goal off an assist, so both are as important as each other."

JADON ON... THE IMPORTANCE OF FAMILY

"They're very happy for me. Even when I went to Dortmund they were very happy with me and they kept on saying: 'just keep working hard and more things will come your way,' and that's what I've been doing. Family is one of the main reasons why I play football, because when I was younger, it was hard growing up. So I do everything for them and I want to keep it that way."

JADON ON... HIS ATTITUDE

"Around the place, it will be serious on the pitch, but also some vibes and a bit of jokes here and there! But definitely when I'm on the pitch it's time to be serious."

EAST STAND

INTRODUCING RAPHAEL VARANE

When Raphael Varane was paraded before United's Premier League opening day victory over Leeds in August 2021, Old Trafford threw open its doors to a serial winner. Having won virtually every available honour with France and Real Madrid, Rapha has certainly made an impression – here are the thoughts of those around him...

"When you say team-mate, he is a true team-mate. We progress together."

PAUL POGBA

"He was really young but, in spite of that, in his eyes, you could see what he wanted, his goals. He wanted to become one of the best centre-backs in the world."

PEPE

"Rapha was young when he arrived. He was a kid but he was very mature. He knew what he was doing, where he was going. He was ready."

MARCELO

"He is always very focused, he is committed and he takes instructions onboard."

ZINEDINE ZIDANE

"He was unknown, but what struck me most was his confidence. Now he's one of the best defenders in the world."

KARIM BENZEMA

"Varane has grown as a player and as a man. He is quick, he has good composure and he is very calm. He accumulated experience at his young age. He is humble and, for me, is one of the best central defenders in the world."

CRISTIANO RONALDO

RAPHA'S HONOURS ROLL

FRANCE
1 X WORLD CUP

REAL MADRID
4 X UEFA CHAMPIONS LEAGUES
4 X FIFA CLUB WORLD CUP
3 X UEFA SUPER CUP
3 X LA LIGA
1 X COPA DEL REY
3 X SPANISH SUPER CUP

"He doesn't think like us. He's different. That's what makes him amazing."

KYLIAN MBAPPE

"Varane is a big-time player. He has all his experience, he's a player who has won a lot during the time of his career at Real Madrid and also in the French national team, so I am sure he will bring all his powers. He really is a top player and I know things are going to go well for him at United."

ANTHONY MARTIAL

"He's an exceptional player and he's proven that over numerous years now and with the trophies he's won. He's a real leader, a winner and to bring him into our defensive unit is really important for options and for competition to make everyone around him improve."

HARRY MAGUIRE

8 GOLDEN RULES

FOR ANY YOUNG PLAYER

MAN UTD

For any United-mad youngster, it's the dream to pull on that famous shirt and represent the Reds. But how can a dream become reality? We spoke with Nick Cox, Head of United's Academy, to get his key pointers for any boy or girl shooting for a career as a professional footballer...

1. WORK HARD & PRACTISE

"ENTHUSIASTIC YOUNG FOOTBALLERS SHOULD PLAY AS MUCH FOOTBALL AS POSSIBLE. PLAY FOR YOUR LOCAL TEAM, IN THE PARK, IN THE PLAYGROUND, IN YOUR GARDEN... WHEREVER YOU CAN FIND AN OPPORTUNITY TO PLAY FOOTBALL, YOU SHOULD PRACTISE, PRACTISE, PRACTISE. DO AS MUCH AS YOU CAN, AS OFTEN AS YOU CAN. THE MORE YOU PLAY, THE MORE OPPORTUNITIES YOU HAVE TO BE SEEN, AND YOU NEVER KNOW WHO MIGHT BE WATCHING YOU AND WHERE THAT MIGHT LEAD. HARD WORK, PRACTISE, DETERMINATION AND COMMITMENT ARE ALL IMPORTANT QUALITIES TO HAVE; IN FACT, A GREAT CHARACTER IS AN ESSENTIAL PART OF REACHING YOUR FULL POTENTIAL. I'VE NEVER SEEN A PLAYER WITH A POOR ATTITUDE REACH THEIR FULL POTENTIAL."

2. PLAY OTHER SPORTS

"IT'S VERY HEALTHY TO TRY OUT A RANGE OF DIFFERENT SPORTS, BECAUSE THEY ALL REQUIRE DIFFERENT SKILLS WHICH COULD ULTIMATELY BE USEFUL IN YOUR FOOTBALL. RIO FERDINAND TRAINED IN BALLET, PHIL NEVILLE PLAYED CRICKET TO A HIGH STANDARD AND THERE ARE LOTS OF OTHER EXAMPLES. TRY AS MANY DIFFERENT SPORTS AS YOU POSSIBLY CAN, EXPERIMENT WITH THINGS THAT YOU MIGHT NOT EXPECT TO LIKE, BECAUSE IT WILL HELP YOU TO LEARN ABOUT YOUR BODY AND UNDERSTAND WHAT YOU'RE CAPABLE OF DOING."

3. LOOK AFTER YOUR BODY

"FOR ANY KIND OF ATHLETE, YOUR BODY IS YOUR MOST IMPORTANT TOOL, SO YOU HAVE TO TAKE CARE OF IT. THAT MEANS THAT YOU HAVE TO STAY WELL HYDRATED, GET PROPER REST, RELAXATION AND SLEEP, PLUS YOU HAVE TO FILL YOURSELF WITH THE RIGHT FOODS MORE OFTEN THAN NOT – THOUGH THERE'S NOTHING WRONG WITH HAVING THE OCCASIONAL BURGER AND ICE CREAM. BEING A KID AND TREATING YOURSELF NOW AND THEN IS AS IMPORTANT AS LOOKING AFTER YOURSELF. WHEN YOU'RE YOUNG, YOU DON'T HAVE TO BEHAVE EXACTLY LIKE A PROFESSIONAL!"

4. EXPRESS YOURSELF

"EVERY PLAYER IS DIFFERENT. EVERYONE HAS DIFFERENT SUPER-STRENGTHS AND YOU WANT TO BE THE BEST VERSION OF YOURSELF THAT YOU CAN BE. IF YOU'RE A PLAYER WHO LOVES TO DRIBBLE PAST OPPONENTS, BE THE BEST DRIBBLER YOU CAN BE. IF YOU'RE A COMPETITOR AND A TOUGH TACKLER, MAKE SURE YOU GIVE 100 PERCENT EVERY TIME YOU PLAY. YOU HAVE TO WORK AT YOUR WEAKNESSES, OF COURSE, BUT IT'S MORE IMPORTANT TO WORK ON YOUR SUPER-STRENGTHS AND REALLY IMPROVE THE THINGS YOU'RE GOOD AT. THAT'S HOW YOU CATCH THE EYE AND CONTRIBUTE TO YOUR TEAM."

8 GOLDEN RULES *FOR ANY YOUNG PLAYER*

5. FOCUS ON YOUR OWN JOURNEY

"DON'T WORRY ABOUT WHAT OTHER PEOPLE ARE UP TO. EVERYBODY'S JOURNEY LOOKS SLIGHTLY DIFFERENT AND PEOPLE WILL DEVELOP AT DIFFERENT RATES. MARCUS RASHFORD STARTED WITH US AT NINE AND CAME ALL THE WAY THROUGH THE ACADEMY, HARRY MAGUIRE JOINED US AS A SENIOR PLAYER HAVING WORKED HIS WAY THROUGH THE LEAGUES AND VARIOUS LOAN SPELLS, BUT BOTH ARE WONDERFUL PLAYERS AND ENGLAND INTERNATIONALS. THERE IS NO SET ROUTE TO THE TOP, SO IF YOU COMPARE YOURSELF TO OTHER PEOPLE THEN YOU'LL ONLY END UP UNHAPPY – THERE WILL ALWAYS BE SOMEONE WHO HAS SOMETHING THAT YOU WANT. LOOK AT YOUR OWN PROGRESS, WORK OUT IF YOU'RE IMPROVING AND THE REAL ART OF SUCCESS IS REACHING YOUR OWN FULL POTENTIAL. GIVING YOUR ALL AND BEING THE BEST THAT YOU CAN BE IS REAL SUCCESS, AND PART OF THAT IS ALSO BEING A GREAT TEAM MEMBER AND HELPING YOUR TEAM-MATES DEVELOP TOO."

6. ENJOY YOURSELF & LOVE THE GAME

"TRY NOT TO PUT TOO MUCH PRESSURE ON YOURSELF. DON'T THINK TOO MUCH ABOUT THE FUTURE, JUST ENJOY THE PRESENT MOMENT. LOVE THE CLUB YOU SUPPORT, LOVE WATCHING YOUR FAVOURITE PLAYERS PLAY AND LOVE GETTING OUT THERE ON THE PITCH, WITH THE BALL AT YOUR FEET, EXPRESSING YOURSELF AND HELPING YOUR TEAM TO THE BEST OF YOUR ABILITIES. IF YOU'RE GOING TO PURSUE A CAREER IN FOOTBALL, YOU HAVE TO LOVE THE SPORT AND THAT WILL HELP DRIVE YOU ALONG THE WAY. TRUE SUCCESS IS KNOWING THAT YOU DID YOUR BEST. QUITE OFTEN, ATTEMPTING TO BECOME A FOOTBALL PLAYER DOESN'T WORK OUT, BUT IT CAN LEAD TO OTHER AMAZING EXPERIENCES. IT ALLOWS YOU TO MAKE NEW FRIENDS AND VISIT DIFFERENT COUNTRIES, IT SHARPENS YOUR PHYSICAL FITNESS AND MENTAL WELLBEING, ALL OF WHICH ARE GREAT ASPECTS OF YOUR DEVELOPMENT. IT CAN ALSO LEAD TO A DIFFERENT CAREER WITHIN FOOTBALL – MAYBE A COACH, A PHYSIO, A MEMBER OF THE MEDIA TEAM... WHO KNOWS? ONE THING THAT IS FOR SURE, THOUGH, IS THAT THE JOURNEY IS MORE IMPORTANT THAN THE DESTINATION."

7. WATCH YOUR ROLE MODELS

"WATCH PLAYERS WHO PLAY IN YOUR POSITION, OR WHO YOU THINK YOU'RE SIMILAR TO IN STYLE, BECAUSE YOU CAN ALWAYS PICK UP TOP TIPS JUST BY WATCHING THEM IN ACTION. TRY TO LOOK AT THEM AS OFTEN AS YOU CAN AND WATCH LOTS OF FOOTBALL IN GENERAL. MAKE SURE YOU TAKE IN AS MANY TIPS AS YOU CAN, BUT ALSO BE SURE TO REMAIN YOURSELF – THE AIM IS ALWAYS TO BE THE BEST VERSION OF YOURSELF, NOT AN IMITATION OF ANOTHER PLAYER."

8. EMBRACE NEW CHALLENGES

"EVERY SINGLE FOOTBALLER HAS HAD DISAPPOINTMENTS DURING THE COURSE OF THEIR CAREER, AND THE VERY BEST PLAYERS ARE THOSE WHO BOUNCE BACK FROM THOSE SETBACKS. WHETHER IT'S NOT BEING SELECTED FOR YOUR TEAM, BEING INJURED, LOSING A GAME OR ANOTHER KIND OF DISAPPOINTMENT, THOSE ARE TYPICAL IN EVERY PLAYER'S DEVELOPMENT AND THEY'RE THE MOST IMPORTANT INGREDIENT IN LEARNING. IT'S IMPORTANT TO REMEMBER THAT SETBACKS ARE WHERE WE LEARN THE MOST ABOUT OURSELVES AND ARE AN IMPORTANT PART OF SUCCESS. SO, JOIN THE TEAM THAT YOU THINK MIGHT BE TOO GOOD FOR YOU, PRACTISE WITH PLAYERS BETTER THAN YOU... FIND A CHALLENGE THAT MAKES YOU NERVOUS AND JUST GO FOR IT."

UNITED

FOCUS ON...

FRED 17

DID YOU KNOW?

RATHER THAN TAKE ON A TRADITIONAL POST-PLAYING CAREER, FRED IS LOOKING TO GO BACK TO UNIVERSITY IN THE FUTURE WHEN HE RETIRES. "MY PARENTS ALWAYS SAID THAT I HAD TO STUDY," HE SAID. "I WOULD REALLY LIKE TO GO BACK. AS SOON AS I RETIRE, I'LL LOOK TO GO BACK OR START AGAIN RATHER. IT'S IMPORTANT WE HAVE KNOWLEDGE IN OUR LIVES."

ON THE IMPORTANCE OF A DEFENSIVE MIDFIELDER:

"MY ROLE IS TO SUPPORT THE ATTACK, FOR THEM TO DO A GOOD JOB, ALSO FOR THE DEFENCE, ON THE BALL. I THINK THIS WORK IS BEING DONE WELL, I'M VERY HAPPY WITH THIS."

FRED

POSITION: MIDFIELDER
BORN: 5 MARCH 1993; BELO HORIZONTE, BRAZIL

Ever since his 2018 arrival from Shakhtar Donetsk, Brazilian midfielder Fred has grown in importance for United. Full of energy, adept at snuffing out opposition build-up play, Fred is a big presence in the Reds' defensive midfield pivot, often as one of a sitting pair. His form for the Reds has also resulted in international recognition, with a starring role in Brazil's Copa America campaign in 2021.

BRUNO FERNANDES

18

"YOU CAN SEE HOW EVERYONE PLAYS WHEN BRUNO'S ON THE PITCH. HE'S CONFIDENT, HE WANTS TO PLAY FORWARD, CREATE CHANCES. HE'S SHARP, QUICK, HARD TO MARK. YOU CAN SEE THAT HE LIFTS EVERYONE. HIM BEING ON THE BALL MAKES OTHERS MAKE RUNS BECAUSE THEY KNOW HE'S CAPABLE OF GIVING THEM THAT BALL."

AARON WAN-BISSAKA, JANUARY 2021

ON HIS WINNING MENTALITY:

"I'D SAY POSSIBLY ONE WORD TO DESCRIBE ME IS 'DEMANDING'. I CAN BE DIFFICULT TO UNDERSTAND WHEN I LOSE — I HAVE A BAD MOOD! THE PEOPLE CLOSEST TO ME KNOW THAT I'M NOT HAPPY WHEN I LOSE. I WAS LIKE IT AS A LITTLE KID AND HAVEN'T CHANGED, SO THEY KNOW HOW TO DEAL WITH ME."

**POSITION: MIDFIELDER
BORN: 8 SEPTEMBER 1994; MAIA, PORTUGAL**

OUR PORTUGUESE MAGNÍFICO

One of the most impactful signings in United's history, Bruno Fernandes has been a revelation since his January 2020 arrival from Sporting Lisbon. A provider of goals and assists galore, the Portugal international midfielder is a natural-born winner who quickly became a fans' favourite, winning the Sir Matt Busby Player of the Season award in 2019/20 and 2020/21!

DID YOU KNOW?

BRUNO'S EAR-CLASPING CELEBRATION IS A SHOUT-OUT TO HIS ELDEST DAUGHTER MATILDE, WHO WOULD OFTEN PUT HER FINGERS IN HER EARS WHEN HER PARENTS WERE TALKING AT HOME!

FANS'
QUESTIONS ANSWERED

PAUL POGBA & LUKE SHAW

Midfield maestro Paul Pogba and flying full-back Luke Shaw are the next duo to face a grilling from United supporters around the world…

PAUL POGBA

WHAT'S YOUR FAVOURITE OTHER SPORT?

ZAIN A (UK)

"My favourite other sport is basketball. Defo basketball. I watch tennis, F1 sometimes. I like ping-pong too as I used to play it."

WHO DID YOU MODEL YOUR GAME ON GROWING UP?

EDWARD M (CANADA)

"I was watching a lot of players. French ones like Thierry Henry, Zinedine Zidane – even Jean-Pierre Papin, I was watching some videos of them. Brazilians Ronaldinho and Ronaldo. Patrick Vieira. Because I was more of a striker before, I was watching the strikers and everything but then I went to no.10, no.6 and no.8 so I started watching everyone. To see what can I improve on in my game, What can I take from all those players, just to make my own, to make Paul Pogba?"

WHO IS THE BEST: MESSI OR RONALDO?

MIN H (MYANMAR)

"It's a nice but trick question as there is no best for me. Two different players. They are two players who both bring joy to watch. Any people are going to have their own opinion of them, just two legends. Me, I would just say they are two legends and not one is better than the other one. Just two people that gives us football players, or football lovers, joy to watch."

HOW DO YOU MANAGE TO STAY SO HAPPY IN GAMES?

MICHAEL O (NIGERIA)

"Football started in the streets, laughing with my friends. That's how I started playing football. So, I mean, smiling or being angry won't change the result. I just feel happy, feel confident when I'm happy on the pitch. That is when I can perform on the pitch the best, just keep smiling, keep believing in myself. After, we will get the result that we want."

HOW WOULD YOU SUM UP YOUR EXPERIENCE AT SCHOOL HERE IN ENGLAND AND HOW IMPORTANT DO YOU THINK IT IS FOR PLAYERS TO GET QUALIFICATIONS AND A GOOD EDUCATION?

NOAH M (UK)

"Unluckily for me, I stopped when I was very young. I was 16 or 17 when I stopped school to follow my dream, in my heart to believe I would become a professional player. But I really wish that I had also had a diploma, and stuff like this, because you never know what is going to happen. But I think with the education you get, you get a lot of education from outside home, which is at school and your friends. You choose your friends and stuff like that and you also finish it at home. I would say you learn at school to be with different people, to be focused, to go somewhere where you want to go and when you want to do something. You go and follow your dream. It's something you have to consider when you're at school, something to push you to follow your dream and go for it. I don't think that is only in sport but also at school. That can help, school can help young kids to go and follow their dream."

WHO IS THE TIDIEST AND UNTIDIEST IN THE DRESSING ROOM?

LUCY R (UK)

"The most tidy is Donny, it's Donny van de Beek and the least tidy is Eric Bailly [laughs]."

FANS'
QUESTIONS ANSWERED

PAUL POGBA & LUKE SHAW

LUKE SHAW

BESIDES A FOOTBALLER WHAT ELSE WOULD YOU DO IF YOU NEVER PLAYED SOCCER?

MARTIN H (IRELAND)

"If I wasn't playing soccer I think I'd probably like to be a police officer. It's a random one but I watch a lot of series and stuff to do with the police and CIA and MI6 and I'm quite into stuff like that, and I think if I wasn't a footballer, I think I'd want to do something based around what they do. So I'd say a police officer."

WHO IS THE FASTEST PLAYER AT MANCHESTER UNITED?

UNITED

ADDI S (JAMAICA)

"I think everyone already knows but it's Daniel James. I saw something once about Deano saying he's the quickest but I wouldn't even put Deano top 10! [Smiles] I don't where that's come from! I'd have to say Daniel James, that's quite an obvious one."

WHAT MUSIC DO YOU LISTEN TO AND HOW DO YOU RELAX?

ANGELA S (UK)

"The music I listen to is hip hop and R&B, especially when I'm relaxing; I like to listen to a bit of R&B and chill on the sofa. How I relax is just chilling on the sofa and not having my little man running about and having me chasing him! [Smiles]"

WHAT WOULD BE YOUR DREAM FIVE-A-SIDE TEAM, INCLUDING ONLY PLAYERS YOU'VE PLAYED ALONGSIDE?

KEANE N (UK)

"This is a very tough question. It's hard this. For my keeper… this is tough because I've played with some very good keepers. I've played with Deano a little bit but not too much so I can't put him in, but he's a brilliant keeper. I think Joe Hart deserves a mention because he was an unbelievable keeper. When I was away with England and played with him I was really impressed with the way he was and the keeper he was, I thought he was absolutely top notch. I'm going to stick with David De Gea in goal and then in defence… this is really hard! [Laughs] I've got to put myself in and then I'll have two in midfield – Wayne Rooney and Paul Pogba and then one left… a striker. Of course, I played with Robin van Persie and he was an unbelievable finisher, but I think I'm going to say, because he's always on the left side with me and I like having him in front of me, I think I'm going to have to say Rashy."

WHO DO YOU CALL FIRST AFTER A WIN?

TAHA H (UK)

"The first person I call after a game is my dad. He's always with my mum anyway so basically I ring them both. I make sure I give my dad a little call after the games to hear his thoughts on the games as he likes to talk about it."

FOCUS ON...

EDINSON CAVANI

"HIS MOVEMENT IN THE BOX IS THE BEST THAT I'VE SEEN AND THE BEST THAT I'VE PLAYED AGAINST. THAT'S WHY HE'S SCORED SO MANY GOALS THROUGHOUT HIS CAREER."

HARRY MAGUIRE, APRIL 2021

ON LEAVING A LEGACY AT OLD TRAFFORD:

"I'D BE HAPPY TO LEAVE THE YOUNGER GUYS HERE WITH SOMETHING WHERE ONE DAY THEY MIGHT SAY: 'EDI WAS LIKE THAT, AND HE DID THIS, AND I LIKED IT AND I TRIED TO COPY ONE OR TWO THINGS.' THAT WOULD BE GREAT. LEAVING SOMETHING POSITIVE BEHIND IS ALWAYS IMPORTANT."

EL MATADOR

POSITION: FORWARD
BORN: 14 FEBRUARY 1987; SALTO, URUGUAY

A free transfer arrival in October 2020, Edinson Cavani spent his first season at United demonstrating how he built a reputation as one of history's finest goalscorers. The veteran Uruguayan bagged a wide range of spectacular goals, but just as important was his exemplary style of play: pouring everything into every performance and always leaving everything out on the field.

DID YOU KNOW?

EDI FAMOUSLY CELEBRATES HIS GOALS BY FIRING AN IMAGINARY ARROW, WHICH IS ACTUALLY A REFERENCE TO THE CHARRÚAS — THE ORIGINAL INHABITANTS OF URUGUAY, CAVANI'S HOME COUNTRY!

21

MASON GREENWOOD

11

"EVERYBODY THINKS MASON IS THE BEST FINISHER AT THE CLUB. GIVE GREENWOOD CHANCES HE WILL SCORE. HE IS DESTINED TO BE A SUPERSTAR. HE'S GOT TO KEEP HIS FEET ON THE GROUND, KEEP WORKING HARD AND THERE'S NOTHING TO STOP HIM."

CLUB LEGEND PAUL SCHOLES

ON CONSTANT DEVELOPMENT:

"I DON'T THINK YOU CAN EVER DO ENOUGH REALLY. ALL THE STUFF YOU CAN GET BETTER AT AND ADD TO YOUR GAME, I DON'T THINK ANYONE IS A COMPLETE FOOTBALLER. THERE ARE ALWAYS LOTS OF THINGS TO IMPROVE ON AND DO BETTER."

POSITION: FORWARD
BORN: 1 OCTOBER 2001;
BRADFORD, ENGLAND

On his rise through the United ranks, there was much excitement about Mason Greenwood's potential. After two full seasons in the Reds' first team, that hype was more than justified. A two-footed, quick-thinking forward blessed with remorseless finishing, Mason established himself as a regular while still in his teens – and the future looks blindingly bright for the England international.

MASON GREENWOOD'S DYNAMITE

AN HISTORIC DAY

FOR UNITED WOMEN!

In March 2021, United Women made history by taking on West Ham United in their first-ever professional game at Old Trafford. Here's how the landmark day unfolded for the Reds…

THE CALM BEFORE THE STORM. THE HOME DRESSING ROOM IS KITTED OUT AHEAD OF AN HISTORIC DAY.

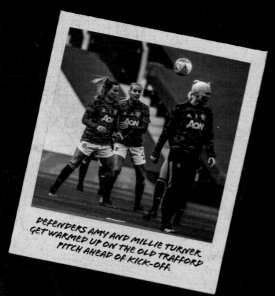

DEFENDERS AMY AND MILLIE TURNER GET WARMED UP ON THE OLD TRAFFORD PITCH AHEAD OF KICK-OFF.

TOP SCORERELLA TOONE TRIES HER LUCK DURING A GOALLESS FIRST HALF.

TAKE ME HOME UNITED ROAD

ONE LOVE

SKIPPER KATIE ZELEM PULLS THE
STRINGS IN MIDFIELD AS THE REDS
LOOK TO FIND A WAY THROUGH.

WITH HER CLEAN SHEET RARELY IN DANGER,
GOALKEEPER MARY EARPS GETS INVOLVED
IN LAUNCHING ANOTHER ATTACK.

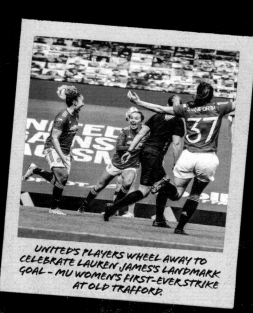

UNITED'S PLAYERS WHEEL AWAY TO
CELEBRATE LAUREN JAMES'S LANDMARK
GOAL – MU WOMEN'S FIRST-EVER STRIKE
AT OLD TRAFFORD.

USA INTERNATIONAL CHRISTEN PRESS
THANKS JACKIE GROENEN FOR HER GREAT
ASSIST AS THE REDS GO 2-0 AHEAD.

A JOB WELL DONE. THE MATCHDAY SQUAD POSE FOR A GROUP
PICTURE TO MARK THE HARD-EARNED 2-0 VICTORY.

MANCHESTER UNITED WOMEN

With Marc Skinner installed as the new manager of Manchester United Women in July 2021, the 2021/22 campaign marked a new chapter in the club's history. Meet the players charged with continuing the Reds' progress of recent seasons...

GOALKEEPERS

27. MARY EARPS

NATIONALITY: ENGLISH
BORN: 7 MARCH 1993

United's first-choice stopper since her 2019 arrival, England international Mary is a key part of the Reds' ambitions. A confident, dominant stopper, she has enjoyed a broad education around the WSL and with two-time Champions League winners VfL Wolfsburg.

32. SOPHIE BAGGALEY

NATIONALITY: ENGLISH
BORN: 27 NOVEMBER 1996

After four seasons of excellent form with Bristol City Ladies, Sophie was signed by the Reds in the summer of 2021. Renowned as one of the best shot-stoppers in the WSL for years, her form has earned her international recognition throughout England's age ladder

DEFENDERS

2. MARTHA HARRIS

NATIONALITY: ENGLISH
BORN: 19 AUGUST 1994

One of the Reds' original squad members from the club's formation in 2018, Martha is a United stalwart who remains one of the best one-v-one defenders around. A full-blooded full-back comfortable on either flank, Harris is an institution within the club.

3. MARIA THORISDOTTIR

NATIONALITY: NORWEGIAN
BORN: 5 JUNE 1993

Signed from Chelsea in 2021, Maria is a highly-decorated, vastly-experienced international who won every honour in English football during her time with the Blues. She also had a two-year break from football between 2012 and 2014 to play handball for Norway!

6. HANNAH BLUNDELL

NATIONALITY: ENGLISH
BORN: 25 MAY 1994

With a raft of top level experience in the Champions League and Super League with Chelsea, Hannah brought invaluable know-how to the Reds' ranks when she arrived in the summer of 2021. A full England international full-back, she provides lung-busting runs up and down the flanks.

5. AOIFE MANNION

NATIONALITY: ENGLISH
BORN: 24 SEPTEMBER 1995

A versatile defender who can play various roles in the backline, Aoife arrived from Manchester City in the summer of 2021. Having represented England up to U23 level, while also sweeping up domestic trophies and playing in the Champions League, she provides key know-how.

17. ONA BATLLE

NATIONALITY: SPANISH
BORN: 10 JUNE 1999

Spanish full-back Ona enjoyed a debut season to remember in her first campaign with the Reds, picking up the club's Player of the Year award for 2020/21. A full-blooded, attack-minded presence at the back, Ona brings real drive to United's approach.

20. KIRSTY SMITH

NATIONALITY: SCOTTISH
BORN: 6 JANUARY 1994

Renowned for her rapid pace, Kirsty is another defender who has been with the Reds since the club's formation. With a hatful of Scotland caps and a wealth of experience, she's a fierce competitor with a sharp football brain.

21. MILLIE TURNER

NATIONALITY: ENGLISH
BORN: 7 JULY 1996

A composed but energetic presence at the heart of defence, Reds stalwart Millie is known to be one of the livelier presences in the United dressing room. While she may be a joker off the pitch, however, she's not one to mess around when the whistle blows!

MAN UTD

MIDFIELDERS

7. ELLA TOONE

NATIONALITY: ENGLISH
BORN: 2 SEPTEMBER 1999

One of the standout players of United's 2020/21 campaign, Ella is a star on the rise. The tricky winger brings pace, purpose and versatility to the Reds' approach, and already has a wealth of international experience with England and Team GB at the Olympics.

8. VILDE BOE RISA

NATIONALITY: NORWEGIAN
BORN: 13 JULY 1995

Brought in from Sandviken in the summer of 2021, Vilde is a Norwegian international with top level pedigree for club and country. A deep-lying playmaker who can run games with her passing, Vilde brings class and calm to the midfield battle.

10. KATIE ZELEM

NATIONALITY: ENGLISH
BORN: 20 JANUARY 1996

Another OG founding member of United Women, Katie Zelem has shone since joining the Reds from Juventus in 2018. A popular and charismatic presence in the squad, it was little surprise that Katie was named captain in 2019 and has continued to lead by example ever since.

11. LEAH GALTON

NATIONALITY: ENGLISH
BORN: 24 MAY 1994

One of the best left wingers around. After spending much of her career playing in America and Germany, Leah joined United in 2018 and quickly established herself as a major attacking threat with her pace and power – especially when unleashing one of her blockbusting shots.

14. JACKIE GROENEN

NATIONALITY: DUTCH
BORN: 17 DECEMBER 1994

A gifted playmaker who has a keen eye for a crafty pass, not to mention a non-stop pressing approach without the ball and crafty, Jackie has been a fixture in United's side since her arrival. The vastly-experienced Dutch international is a key part of the Reds' attacking patterns.

12. HAYLEY LADD

NATIONALITY: WELSH
BORN: 6 OCTOBER 1993

United's first Welsh player joined the club in 2019 and soon demonstrated her sharp reading of the game with a string of impressive displays in a midfield holding role, but she remains versatile enough to shine almost anywhere on the field.

18. KIRSTY HANSON

NATIONALITY: SCOTTISH
BORN: 17 APRIL 1998

Blessed with sublime delivery of the ball from the wings, Scotland international Kirsty has brought graft and power to the flanks since joining in 2018. A true team player who would run through brick walls for the greater good.

24. CARRIE JONES

NATIONALITY: WELSH
BORN: 4 SEPTEMBER 2003

When a player makes her full international debut at the age of just 15, you know she's a special talent. Teenage midfielder Carrie has been turning heads throughout her short career so far, with her calm, two-footed approach underpinned by a super-mature work ethic.

37. LUCY STANIFORTH

NATIONALITY: ENGLISH
BORN: 2 OCTOBER 1992

A full England international with a wealth of top flight experience, Lucy joined United from Birmingham City in 2020 and swiftly set about demonstrating the classy midfield play which prompted the Reds to sign her.

FORWARDS

9. MARTHA THOMAS

NATIONALITY: SCOTTISH
BORN: 31 MAY 1996

A former USA youth international during her time living in the States, Martha was also eligible to play for England and Scotland, ultimately deciding on the latter. A natural-born finisher, Thomas joined the Reds in 2021 after spells with Le Havre and West Ham.

23. ALESSIA RUSSO

NATIONALITY: ENGLISH
BORN: 8 FEBRUARY 1999

One of English football's top young attacking prospects, United fan Alessia joined the Reds in 2020 after excelling in college soccer in America. Having already received a senior England cap, the gifted young forward is preparing to burst to prominence with her childhood team.

13. IVANA FERREIRA FUSO

NATIONALITY: BRAZIL
BORN: 12 MARCH 2001

Brazilian-born but raised in Germany, Ivana joined United in 2020 and found her early months in England hampered by injury. She fought her way back to full fitness, however, and earned a senior Brazil call-up for her efforts.

ESPORTS

ELDRIDGE O'NIEL

WHAT'S IT LIKE TO BE A PRO GAMER... FOR UNITED?

There are dream jobs, and then there's being a member of the Manchester United eSports team! Formed in 2019, the small but dedicated squad comprises three pro gamers who represent the Reds in international eFootball tournaments. We caught up with team captain Eldridge O'Niel to shed light on one of life's great careers…

ELDRIDGE, TELL US WHAT IT FEELS LIKE TO BE A MANCHESTER UNITED ESPORTS PLAYER...

It's a very special feeling. I'm honoured. The first time I spoke to the club, I couldn't believe that they were interested in signing me. It's like being part of a big family. The first time I came to Old Trafford to talk with Scott Martin, our manager, and the team, everyone just immediately made it feel like home and that this is the right place to be. This is a huge thing for me and I can't even explain how special it feels to be part of the biggest club in the world. When I tell people that I'm a pro gamer for Manchester United, people are always so shocked. Their eyes go huge!

YOUR BROTHER GYLIANO VAN VELZEN WAS A UNITED PLAYER BETWEEN 2010 AND 2013 – HOW DID HE REACT WHEN YOU TOLD HIM THAT YOU WERE FOLLOWING IN HIS FOOTSTEPS?

My brother was in the team that won the FA Youth Cup so, when I told him eight years later that I was playing for the club, he was like: "WHAT??" He couldn't believe it! Gyliano made it to United, my other brother made it to Ajax, both as professional footballers, now I'm an esports player for United and the Dutch national team, so I tell them that we've all done the same thing – even if it's a game!

YOUR FAMILY MUST BE SO PROUD OF SUCH A UNIQUE SIBLING SITUATION WHERE YOU'VE BOTH REPRESENTED THE CLUB...

For sure. My mother would always tell me when I was younger: "Stop gaming, you're gaming too much – go learn lessons, go to school, go earn money!" Then last year she said it to me again and I said: "Mum, this is my work now." She is proud and everyone in my family is too. My younger brother says he looks up to me and how I don't let anything disturb me or distract me from what I want when I'm training. That's how it's supposed to be, even if it's esports. When you're doing what you want to do and you want to achieve something, you have to be in love with the game and let nothing distract you.

TELL US ABOUT YOUR TEAM-MATES...

We have Kamel, the vice-captain. He's a French player, one of the best in Europe – in the top 10 in 1v1 games, definitely – and in France the level is high. He always does well on European stages. He's mentally very strong, he knows a lot about the game, his passion for the game is off the charts! Very emotional player, great skills, whatever you need to know about the game, he knows. Then we have Mikolaj, who came into the team as a 16-year-old who had just started and I could see his potential even then. He'd played one tournament in his career but United saw the potential in him and since signing, he's been runner-up at two big tournaments. He's ice cold. We call him the silent assassin. He improved a lot from when he joined the team, so I would say that, like Kamel, he's also definitely top 10 in Europe right now. Now he plays different formations and approaches. Between the three of us, we have a versatile team, and with Kamel and I being so emotional and passionate, Mikolaj balances it out by being calm and composed. It's a very good mix. The three of us represent Manchester United to the best of our abilities and we are like brothers now. We have known each other for a few years now and we look after each other.

ESPORTS

SINCE THE ESPORTS TEAM WAS FORMED, HOW HAVE THE CLUB SUPPORTED THE PLAYERS?

I couldn't ask for any more from the club. I wanna bet that the management team behind us is the best you can get. From day one we had a training camp where you could meet the staff, bond with each other and everything was done for us. Hotels, daily training, food, it was all arranged for us and we were laughing with each other, saying: "This is the life!" We've played in places like Barcelona and had everything taken care of for us – tickets, clothing, everything. When the pandemic started, we began video meetings to catch up every week to talk through everything. We gamed in online competitions instead, we were able to create content with players and legends like Scott McTominay, Tahith Chong and Louis Saha. We were so happy with what the club did for us. We've even been able to speak to coaches about the mental side of our performances, how we feel, how to perform better. We are free to talk about what we want and how we feel. It feels like you're talking to trustworthy people without being judged or held accountable, so we really feel at home at this club. They're even helping us to boost our profile, helping us on social media. United is the biggest club in the world, but the team behind it is incredible.

IN TERMS OF EFOOTBALL, WHO'S YOUR FAVOURITE UNITED PLAYER IN THE GAME?

Marcus Rashford is our key player. He's quick, strong, he scores a lot of goals for us and he's pretty tall as well. Last season we also liked Harry Maguire a lot because he's big, tall, good centre-back. Bruno is very important because he has good passing skills and is a strong corner-taker. We like the quick, pacey players upfront like Rashford, Greenwood, Martial… D'Mani Mellor from the Academy has been a key player because of his speed. The game is about pace and physical strength.

WHAT ARE YOUR PREFERRED TACTICS AND FORMATION?

The best is 4-3-3, but not how the Dutch play, because the Dutch play with wingers. In this game you can slide your players to certain positions, so most gamers on eFootball slide their players centrally, so you end up with three centre-forwards in a narrow formation. A lot of the game is played down the middle, so it pays to do that. That means that defensively you can play four centre-backs, which blocks all counters against you. That's better than having wing-backs because they can go up and leave you with just two players at the back, which is too dangerous.

FINALLY, ELDRIDGE, WHAT ARE YOUR KEY TIPS FOR ANYBODY LOOKING TO MAKE A CAREER IN PRO GAMING?

Besides being crazy about the game and making sure you don't let things disturb you, you have to make sure you eat well – nutrition is very important – and rest as well. Some people play too much and overplaying can work against you. It can affect your style of play because you end up overthinking. It's important to know when to stop, when to eat, when to go to bed, when to do something else because it's not all about gaming non-stop.

A DAY IN THE LIFE

ELDRIDGE WALKS US THROUGH THE DAILY ROUTINE OF A PRO GAMER...

"Most of the time I'll clean the house a bit after I wake up, then play 1v1 by myself in eFootball. Then I'll take a nap because I need to be refreshed for my training session in the afternoon. You need to treat training like a matchday. Usually that's four hours of training against an opponent who is also a professional team, after that for me it's quality time with the kids, put them to bed, eat, then maybe a box set or a movie and go to bed. Sometimes, after we've finished training, I'll play some more eFootball, but basically this is what my day looks like. I don't put a cap on how much I'll play in a day, it depends how I feel. If I feel like I can play five or six hours then I do, but if I feel myself getting tired and my focus is dropping, that means the chances of losing are increasing and I HATE to lose, so I stop playing!"

MEET THE
LITTLE DEVILS

ZAC

CHARLIE

Midway through 2021, two new young stars emerged at Old Trafford. That's hardly shocking, given United's record at producing fledgling talents, but these lads aren't part of the United squad – they're the Little Devils, AKA Zac and Charlie. As new additions to the club's team of reporters, they've already grilled Ole and a number of first-team stars, as well as a series of club legends and they've got their sights set on pinning down even more for questioning in the future. We turned the tables, though, and managed to ask THEM a few questions on a wide range of topics. Let's get to know the Little Devils…

FIRSTLY BOYS, WHO ARE YOUR FAVOURITE UNITED PLAYERS?

ZAC   I've got three or four – I love Aaron Wan-Bissaka, Marcus Rashford, Bruno Fernandes and Edinson Cavani.

CHARLIE   I love Cavani, Fernandes, Jesse Lingard and Aaron Wan-Bissaka… and I also love Rashford.

UNITED

WHEN YOU PLAY FOOTBALL, WHAT POSITION DO YOU EACH PREFER?

ZAC   Central attacking midfielder always for me. The position Fernandes plays. I do play in goal at times, but CAM is my position. I don't score too much, but I can provide a lot of assists.

CHARLIE   I like left wing. I like to win too.

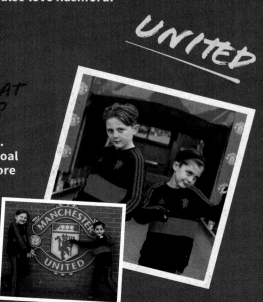

ZAC

HOW WOULD YOU DESCRIBE EACH OTHER AS PLAYERS?

ZAC I have to say Charlie is Roy Keane! [Laughs] There is no mercy. If the opposition score he shouts at everyone. He's very, very vocal!

CHARLIE Zac likes to score goals. He's a good player, but I think he's a better goalie than an outfield player.

LITTLE DEVILS

WHAT'S THE BEST THING ABOUT BEING LITTLE DEVILS REPORTERS?

ZAC We feel so lucky to be able to interview these incredible players who we love – it feels like a dream. When I do an interview I feel like I am asleep dreaming because it's so amazing for us.

CHARLIE It's just amazing. Some kids that support United don't get the chance to do this and the fact that me and Zac have had the opportunity is amazing and we feel so lucky.

CHARLIE

WHAT DO YOUR FAMILY AND FRIENDS THINK ABOUT IT?

ZAC Not all my friends are United fans – no idea why! My family are really proud and they know how much United means to me so to have the chance to do this is amazing.

CHARLIE They're proud of me and they have enjoyed the interviews so far.

IS WORKING IN FOOTBALL SOMETHING YOU'D LIKE TO DO FOREVER?

ZAC Oh yes. Absolutely. I'd love to be a footballer, then a manager and if I get sacked I'd like to become an owner until I get another team to manage!

CHARLIE I'd like to be no.7 forever because all these fantastic players like Cristiano Ronaldo, Bryan Robson, David Beckham, Eric Cantona and Edinson Cavani have been no.7. And then… one day… it's going to be me! [Laughs]

WHICH HAS BEEN YOUR FAVOURITE INTERVIEW SO FAR?

ZAC
To interview Ole was just amazing. Interviewing the Manchester United manager is a dream for us and he was brilliant to us. Every interview has been brilliant, but three of my other favourites were... in no particular order but these have been my favourites! It would be Juan Mata, Denis Irwin and Bryan Robson. He took forever on our 'In A Rush' round but he said that was because he lives in a mansion! [Laughs]

CHARLIE
Like Zac said interviewing Ole was just incredible. We were so lucky to chat to him. We had the best day and he gave us some great answers and we loved 'In A Rush' with him and the kitman Bucks! I have loved every single interview.

BIGGEST THING YOU'VE LEARNT AS REPORTERS?

ZAC
That's a hard question. I've learnt so much... I learn that me and Charlie can't talk at the same time! [Laughs]

CHARLIE
I learnt not to ask about City – no-one wants to talk about them except for when we beat them! [Laughs]

CHARLIE

WHAT'S THE ONE THING YOU'VE BEEN TOLD DURING AN INTERVIEW WHICH HAS SURPRISED YOU THE MOST?

ZAC
When Lee Grant told us Dean Henderson was the messiest player in the dressing room. I thought Dean would be really tidy, but Lee said he wasn't!

CHARLIE
I was shocked in the Lee Grant interview that Paul Pogba was the noisiest. I know he likes to dance, but when he's interviewed he's quite quiet! We can't wait to interview him!

YOU GOT TO PLAY ON THE OLD TRAFFORD PITCH AND SCORE AT THE STRETFORD END – WHAT WAS THAT EXPERIENCE LIKE?

ZAC

ZAC
It was the best feeling ever. That moment when I kicked the ball into the goal at the Stretford End I pretended a million people watching and celebrating – it was better than I could have imagined!

CHARLIE
It was one of the greatest experiences of my life! Hardly anyone gets to play on the pitch – it felt very special.

ZAC

WHAT HAS BEEN YOUR FAVOURITE MOMENT OF THE SERIES SO FAR?

ZAC
My favourite round is 'In A Rush'! Dwight Yorke was quick but he lives in a flat! Lee Grant was probably my favourite because he filmed it around Carrington so we got to see behind the scenes! Ole's In A Rush with Bucks the kitman is a must-watch – it was brilliant!

CHARLIE
In the Juan Mata interview when Juan and I were joking about how to say Jonny Evans' name in a Spanish accent. It was so funny!

WHAT ONE QUESTION WOULD YOU LOVE TO ASK EACH OTHER?

ZAC
I have two... why are you like Roy Keane and why do you always try to nutmeg and always fail?

CHARLIE
My question for Zac is what position would he play because I'm confused as to which is his best – goalkeeper or CAM?

FINALLY BOYS, WHO IS YOUR DREAM INTERVIEWEE AND WHAT WOULD BE YOUR FIRST QUESTION FOR THEM?

ZAC
I'd love to interview Cristiano Ronaldo and I'd ask: 'Please tell us you're coming back to United, Cristiano?!'

CHARLIE
Sir Alex and I would ask him which player was the most important in helping us win the Treble.

CHARLIE

SEND THE BOYS YOUR QUESTIONS!

Watch all the latest episodes of Little Devils and submit your questions for Zac and Charlie to ask in their future interviews!

VISIT:
MANUTD.COM/LITTLEDEVILS

QUIZZES & PUZZLES

2020/21 REVISITED

Were you paying attention last season? Let's see how you get on with 20 teasers from last term...

1. AGAINST WHICH TEAM DID THE REDS' PREMIER LEAGUE CAMPAIGN BEGIN?

2. WHO SCORED THE FIRST GOAL OF UNITED'S SEASON?

3. WHAT WAS UNIQUE ABOUT BRUNO FERNANDES'S WINNER AT BRIGHTON?

4. WHICH FORMER PSG STRIKER JOINED UNITED IN OCTOBER 2020?

5. ANOTHER NEW SIGNING MADE HIS REDS DEBUT AGAINST PSG – WHO WAS IT?

6. WHAT SCORE DID UNITED BEAT RB LEIPZIG AT OLD TRAFFORD?

7. WHO SCORED HIS FIRST SENIOR HAT-TRICK IN THAT GAME?

8. WHICH RED SET A PREMIER LEAGUE RECORD BY SCORING TWICE IN THE FIRST THREE MINUTES AGAINST LEEDS?

9. WHO DID UNITED KNOCK OUT OF THE LEAGUE CUP QUARTER-FINALS TWO DAYS BEFORE CHRISTMAS?

ANSWERS ON PAGE 60

10. WHICH PLAYER SCORED THE REDS' FIRST GOAL OF 2021, WITH THE OPENER AGAINST ASTON VILLA?

11. WHICH TEAM DID UNITED BEAT IN THE THIRD ROUND OF THE FA CUP?

12. IN JANUARY, WHO SCORED THE REDS' WINNING GOALS AT BURNLEY AND FULHAM?

13. WHO ARRIVED AT OLD TRAFFORD AS A NEW SIGNING IN THE JANUARY TRANSFER WINDOW?

14. WHAT WAS THE FINAL SCORE IN UNITED'S FA CUP MEETING WITH LIVERPOOL?

15. HOW MANY UNITED PLAYERS SCORED IN THE 9-0 WIN OVER SOUTHAMPTON?

16. THE DEMOLITION OF SOUTHAMPTON EQUALLED THE REDS' PL RECORD WIN AGAINST WHICH TEAM IN 1995?

17. WHO WAS THE UNLIKELY GOALSCORER OF UNITED'S SECOND GOAL IN THE 2-0 WIN AT MANCHESTER CITY?

18. WHAT WAS THE AGGREGATE SCORE IN THE REDS' EUROPA LEAGUE WIN OVER ROMA?

19. WHO SCORED THE FINAL GOAL OF UNITED'S PREMIER LEAGUE SEASON, WITH A PENALTY AT WOLVES?

20. WHICH PLAYER FINISHED ON TOP OF THE REDS' SCORING CHARTS FOR 2020/21 WITH 28 GOALS?

ANSWERS ON PAGE 60

FIND THE AWARD WINNERS

Can you spot 10 names of players who have won the
Sir Matt Busby Player of the Year award?

WORDSEARCH

```
U G K I K I E B E C K H A M
B N D N H D M T I A R I N V
Q A S C U U O A N O G E Z U
C E Y E N O O R B R N D E A
U G R G O E A S N O L F Y R
O E N C E U O N C F O E T O
Z D G U A N X R S E I R E N
Q Z F Y M N G E Y E Y N A A
Y O O R L E T S I N N A V L
A G V I R J X O U I M N E D
A K T M F H W E N T W D Z O
Y O T M Z H O E N A Z E F U
K E A N E M A E N R B S I D
```

FERNANDES   RONALDO   DE GEA   CANTONA   KEANE

VAN NISTELROOY   ROONEY   ROBSON   BECKHAM   INCE

NAME THE SQUAD MEMBERS

Which of United's current players could make the following statements?

1. I JOINED UNITED FROM VILLARREAL IN 2016

2. I MADE MY COMPETITIVE REDS DEBUT AT PARIS ST GERMAIN IN 2019

3. BEFORE SCOTT McTOMINAY WORE IT, MY SQUAD NUMBER WAS 39

4. I SCORED ON MY UNITED DEBUT AGAINST CHELSEA

5. I BEGAN MY CAREER AS AN OUTFIELD PLAYER AT CARLISLE, BEFORE BECOMING A GOALKEEPER

6. BEFORE JOINING UNITED, I BECAME PSG'S ALL-TIME LEADING GOALSCORER

7. AS A YOUNGSTER, I HAD TO CHOOSE BETWEEN PLAYING PROFESSIONAL FOOTBALL OR ICE HOCKEY

8. I WAS BORN IN BELO HORIZONTE, BRAZIL

9. AS A YOUTH TEAM PLAYER AT CRYSTAL PALACE, I WAS A WINGER

10. I PLAYED AGAINST UNITED IN THE 2010/11 FA YOUTH CUP FINAL

THE ROAD TO OLD TRAFFORD

Can you match each player to their previous club and the year of their transfer to United?

1. PORTO, 2018	ERIC CANTONA
2. NEWCASTLE UNITED, 1995	DALEY BLIND
3. SPORTING LISBON, 2003	ANTHONY MARTIAL
4. AJAX, 2014	ANDY COLE
5. BLACKBURN ROVERS, 2011	CRISTIANO RONALDO
6. MONACO, 2015	PHIL JONES
7. NOTTINGHAM FOREST, 1993	DAVID DE GEA
8. LEEDS UNITED, 1992	ROY KEANE
9. ATLETICO MADRID, 2011	DIOGO DALOT
10. PSG, 2016	ZLATAN IBRAHIMOVIC

GOAL OR NO GOAL?

United's players scored a combined 121 goals in 2020/21. Of the eight efforts pictured below, five resulted in goals and three didn't – can you identify them?

BRUNO V EVERTON

RASHFORD V BRIGHTON

CAVANI V EVERTON

BRUNO V LIVERPOOL

GREENWOOD V BURNLEY

FRED V NEWCASTLE

POGBA V AC MILAN

GREENWOOD V LEICESTER

ANSWERS ON PAGE 60

WHICH UNITED PLAYER ARE YOU?

Take our personality test to determine which outfield player you most think like...

1. WHAT'S YOUR FAVOURITE THING ABOUT FOOTBALL?

a) Scoring from long-range
b) Out-running everybody else
c) Making the perfect tackle
d) Scoring a goal from absolutely nothing

2. HOW FAST ARE YOU ON THE PITCH?

a) One of the faster players out there
b) Greased lightning, nobody's catching me
c) Quick enough, especially when I think faster than everyone else
d) Fleet-footed, even with the ball at my feet

3. HOW WOULD YOU DESCRIBE YOUR PLAYING STYLE?

a) String-puller
b) Up and down the pitch, non-stop
c) One step ahead of the opponent
d) Totally unpredictable

4. YOU'RE TAKING A PENALTY KICK – WHAT'S GOING THROUGH YOUR MIND?

a) I'll flummox the keeper with my crafty run-up
b) Bottom corner, all day long
c) BASH! Time to rip the net out
d) Hmm, which foot should I use?

5. WHAT COLOUR BOOTS ARE YOU LIKELY TO WEAR?

a) Burnt orange
b) Light gold
c) Pure white
d) Deep red

6. WHEN YOU'RE PLAYING, HOW MUCH OF A TALKER ARE YOU?

a) I'm always talking to everybody around me
b) I share my thoughts when I need to
c) I finish every game with a sore throat
d) I tend to let my feet do the talking

ANSWERS ON PAGE 60

It's time to see how well you know United

2020/21 REVISITED

1. Crystal Palace
2. Donny van de Beek
3. It was a penalty awarded by VAR after the final whistle
4. Edinson Cavani
5. Alex Telles
6. 5-0
7. Marcus Rashford
8. Scott McTominay
9. Everton
10. Anthony Martial
11. Watford
12. Paul Pogba
13. Amad Diallo
14. 3-2 to United
15. Seven
16. Ipswich Town
17. Luke Shaw
18. 8-5 to United
19. Juan Mata
20. Bruno Fernandes

WORD SEARCH

```
U G K I K I E B E C K H A M M
B N D N H D M T I A R I N V
Q A S C U U O A N O G E Z U
C E Y E N O O R B R N D E A
U G R G O E A S N O L F Y R
O E N C E U O N C F O E T O
Z D G U A N X R S E I R N N
Q Z F Y M N G E Y E Y N A A
Y O O R L E T S I N N A V L
A G V I R J X O U I M N E D
A K T M F H W E N T W N D Z O
Y O T M Z H O E N A Z E F U
K E A N E M A E N R B S I D
```

NAME THE SQUAD MEMBER...

1. Eric Bailly
2. Mason Greenwood
3. Marcus Rashford
4. Daniel James
5. Dean Henderson
6. Edinson Cavani
7. Victor Lindelof
8. Fred
9. Aaron Wan-Bissaka
10. Harry Maguire

MAN UTD

THE ROAD TO OLD TRAFFORD

1. Porto, 2018 – Diogo Dalot
2. Newcastle United, 1995 – Andy Cole
3. Sporting Lisbon, 2003 – Cristiano Ronaldo
4. Ajax, 2014 – Daley Blind
5. Blackburn Rovers, 2011 – Phil Jones
6. Monaco, 2015 – Anthony Martial
7. Nottingham Forest, 1993 – Roy Keane
8. Leeds United, 1992 – Eric Cantona
9. Atletico Madrid, 2011 – David De Gea
10. PSG, 2016 – Zlatan Ibrahimovic

GOAL OR NO GOAL?

A. Rashford v Brighton – Goal
B. Bruno v Everton - No goal
C. Cavani v Everton - Goal
D. Bruno v Liverpool – Goal
E. Greenwood v Burnley - No goal
F. Greenwood v Leicester – Goal
G. Pogba v AC Milan – Goal
H. Fred v Newcastle - No goal

WHICH UNITED PLAYER ARE YOU?

Mostly A. Bruno Fernandes
Mostly B. Luke Shaw
Mostly C. Harry Maguire
Mostly D. Mason Greenwood

UNITED

COMPETITION TIME!

We've got a 2021/22 United shirt signed by first team members, to be won by one lucky reader.

To be in with a shout, just answer this straightforward question:

WHICH PLAYER WON THE 2020/21 SIR MATT BUSBY PLAYER OF THE YEAR AWARD?

A. LUKE SHAW

B. BRUNO FERNANDES

C. EDINSON CAVANI

TO ENTER, JUST VISIT MANUTD.COM/ANNUAL2022

GOOD LUCK!